W9-CEU-557

PUSHCART

THE COOK'S QUOTATION BOOK

The Cook's Quotation Book

A literary feast

PUSHCART

EDITED BY

MARIA POLUSHKIN ROBBINS

FIRST PRINTING OCTOBER, 1983

Copyright © 1983 by Maria Polushkin Robbins
All rights reserved, which includes the right to reproduce this
book or portions thereof in any form whatsoever, without
written permission of the publisher. For information address
The Pushcart Press, P.O. Box 380, Wainscott, New York 11975.

ISBN: 0-916366-19-7

MANUFACTURED IN THE UNITED STATES OF AMERICA
by Ray Freiman & Company

This book is the felicitous result of the two great and guilty pleasures of my life—eating and reading. What nostalgia I have about my childhood years has to do with the extravagant indulgence of these two happy vices. Alas, never again will there be so much time, so much leisure to curl up and read on and on, devouring books with such innocent greed. And, never again either can eating be approached with such careless abandon—for now in my forties a candy bar is as rare a luxury as a pound of caviar, and buttered toast or a fried egg must be worked off in aerobic agony.

But I recall so clearly the pleasure of my first encounter with certain passages of, say, The Wind in the Willows. *Do you remember breaking the code of, "coldtonguecoldhamcoldbeefpickledgherkinssaladfrenchrollscresssandwichespottedmeatgingerbeerlemonadesodawater—"? There I was feeling so clever and suddenly so hungry, and I very much agreed with Mole who cried out in ecstasies, "Stop, stop. This is too much!" For years I carried around in my head the description, which comes later on in the same book, of a picnic basket which held a long French bread, a garlic sausage, and "some cheese which lay down and cried..." so that fully a decade later when first I encountered a wedge of ripe brie,*

I recognized it instantly as the very same weepy cheese. It is this connection between the literary and the culinary that I have always found irresistible.

Of course you remember the scene in A Little Princess *where poor Sara, having gone hungry for days and days, (even now I feel the sympathetic hunger pangs) wakes up in her garret to find a sumptuous surprise supper laid out for her... And the scene in* Tom Sawyer *when Huck and Tom, also hungry, as hungry as two growing boys ever were, caught some fish and fried them with bacon over a campfire for their breakfast...*

And there are scenes in Dickens, and James Joyce and Trollope, and Rex Stout and Lewis Carroll and Herman Melville and Dorothy Sayers and Virginia Woolf and Colette... and Proust, naturally. And I could go on and on, and did for many evenings around our dinner table and the dinner tables of others, until it was decided to collect these culinary moments and bon mots of literature in this book.

So many people helped, foraging through their reading/eating memories, but I would especially like to thank Bill Henderson, who responded to my idea with such alacrity and grace; Genie Chipps for reminding me of poor Scarlett O'Hara's famous pledge; Michael Disher, who generously shared his vast knowledge of the movies; Pat Strachan for so many valuable suggestions; Andy Weil for many esoteric sources; John Ford for his impeccable taste; Winnie Rosen for being there; and most of all my husband Ken who often has to eat beans because I'm reading about roast beef.

MARIA POLUSHKIN ROBBINS
East Hampton, New York

THE COOK'S QUOTATION BOOK

Next to eating good dinners, a healthy man with a benev-
olent turn of mind, must like, I think, to read about them.
WILLIAM MAKEPEACE THACKERAY

I look upon it, that he who does not mind his belly will
hardly mind anything else.
SAMUEL JOHNSON

> We may live without poetry, music and
> art;
> We may live without conscience and live
> without heart;
> We may live without friends; we may
> live without books;
> But civilized man cannot live without
> cooks.
> He may live without books,—what is
> knowledge but grieving?
> He may live without hope,—what is
> hope but deceiving?
> He may live without love,—what is
> passion but pining?
> But where is the man that can live
> without dining?
> OWEN MEREDITH

Grub first, then ethics.
BRECHT

We must eat to live and live to eat.
HENRY FIELDING

There is a communion of more than our bodies when bread is broken and wine is drunk. And that is my answer, when people ask me: Why do you write about hunger, and not wars or love.

M. F. K. FISHER

Life is so brief that we should not glance either too far backwards or forwards ... therefore study how to fix our happiness in our glass and in our plate.

GRIMOD DE LA REYNIERE

... a good meal in troubled times is always that much salvaged from disaster.

A. J. LIEBLING

If a man be sensible and one fine morning, while he is lying in bed, count at the tips of his fingers how many things in this life truly will give him enjoyment, invariably he will find food is the first one.

LIN YUTANG

No restaurants. The means of consoling oneself: reading cookbooks.

BAUDELAIRE

Gazing at the typewriter in moments of desperation, I console myself with three thoughts: alcohol at six, dinner at eight and to be immortal you've got to be dead.

GYLES BRANDETH

Looks can be deceiving—it's eating that's believing.
JAMES THURBER

There is a charm in improvised eating which a regular meal lacks, and there was a glamour never to be recaptured in secret picnics on long sunny mornings on the roof of the Hall... I would sit up there with my cousin Tooter, consuming sweets bought with our weekly pocket money and discussing possible futures... The sweets I remember best were white and tubular, much thinner than any cigarette, filled with a dark chocolate filling. If I found one now I am sure that it would have the taste of hope.
GRAHAM GREENE

What is sauce for the goose may be sauce for the gander, but it is not necessarily sauce for the chicken, the duck, the turkey or the Guinea hen.
ALICE B. TOKLAS

Madam, I have been looking for a person who disliked gravy all my life: let us swear eternal friendship.
SYDNEY SMITH

A man's own dinner is to himself so important that he cannot bring himself to believe that it is a matter utterly indifferent to anyone else.
ANTHONY TROLLOPE

The way to a man's heart is through his stomach.
FANNY FERN

Leopold Bloom ate with relish the inner organs of beasts
and fowls. He liked thick giblet soup, nutty gizzards, a
stuffed roast heart, liver slices fried with breadcrumbs,
fried hencod's roe. Most of all he liked grilled mutton
kidneys which gave to his palate a fine tang of scented
urine.

JAMES JOYCE

A man is in general better pleased when he has a good
dinner upon the table than when his wife talks Greek.

SAMUEL JOHNSON

Serenely full the Epicure may say—
Fate cannot harm me—I have dined today.

SYDNEY SMITH

All human history attests
That happiness for man—the hungry sinner!
Since Eve ate apples, much depends on dinner.

LORD BYRON

The discovery of a new dish does more for the happiness
of mankind than the discovery of a star.

BRILLAT-SAVARIN

Thought depends absolutely on the stomach, but in spite
of that, those who have the best stomachs are not the best
thinkers.

VOLTAIRE

When ordering lunch the big executives are just as indecisive as the rest of us.

WILLIAM FEATHER

No man can be wise on an empty stomach.

GEORGE ELIOT

Life is a banquet and most poor suckers are starving!

ROSALIND RUSSELL in the movie
Auntie Mame

There is no love sincerer than the love of food.

GEORGE BERNARD SHAW

"There's cold chicken inside it," replied the Rat briefly; "coldtonguecoldhamcoldbeefpickled-gherkinssaladfrenchrollscresssandwichespotted-meatgingerbeerlemonadesodawater—"

"Oh stop, stop," cried the Mole in ecstasies: "This is too much!"

KENNETH GRAHAME

Let me smile with the wise, and feed with the rich.

SAMUEL JOHNSON

Soup and fish explain half the emotions of life.

SYDNEY SMITH

Beautiful soup! Who cares for fish, game, or any other dish? Who would not give all else for two pennyworth only of beautiful soup?

LEWIS CARROLL

Do you have a kinder, more adaptable friend in the food world than soup? Who soothes you when you are ill? Who refuses to leave you when you are impoverished and stretches its resources to give you a hearty sustenance and cheer? Who warms you in the winter and cools you in the summer? Yet who is also capable of doing honor to your richest table and impressing your most demanding guests? . . . Soup does its loyal best, no matter what undignified conditions are imposed upon it. But soup knows the difference. Soup is sensitive. You don't catch steak hanging around when you're poor and sick, do you?

JUDITH MARTIN
aka Miss Manners

Of soup and love, the first is best.

SPANISH PROVERB

Of all the items on the menu, soup is that which exacts the most delicate perfection and the strictest attention.

ESCOFFIER

Noncooks think it's silly to invest two hours' work in two minutes' enjoyment; but if cooking is evanescent, well, so is the ballet.

JULIA CHILD

If you throw a lamb chop in the oven, what's to keep it from getting done?
  JOAN CRAWFORD
  in the movie *The Women*

But when that smoking chowder came in, the mystery was delightfully explained. Oh! sweet friends, hearken to me. It was made of small juicy clams, scarcely bigger than hazelnuts, mixed with pounded ship's biscuits and salted pork cut up into little flakes! the whole enriched with butter, and plentifully seasoned with pepper and salt . . . we despatched it with great expedition.
  HERMAN MELVILLE

This is not that, and that certainly is not this, and at the same time an oyster stew is not stewed, and although they are made of the same things and even cooked almost the same way, an oyster soup should never be called a stew, nor stew soup.
  M. F. K. FISHER

Cuisine is when things taste like themselves.
  CURNONSKY

In cooking, as in all the arts, simplicity is the sign of perfection.
  CURNONSKY

In the vegetable world, there is nothing so innocent, so confiding in its expression, as the small green face of the freshly shelled spring pea. Asparagus is pushing and bossy, lettuce is loud and blowsy, radishes are gay and playful, but the little green pea is so helpless and friendly that it makes really sensitive stomachs suffer to see how he is treated in the average home. Fling him into the water and let him boil—and that's that.

WILLIAM WALLACE IRWIN

Progress in civilization has been accompanied by progress in cookery.

FANNIE FARMER

An army marches on its stomach.

NAPOLEON I

A chicken in every pot.

HERBERT HOOVER

You cannot feed the hungry on statistics.

DAVID LLOYD GEORGE

When my mother had to get dinner for eight she'd just make enough for sixteen and only serve half.

GRACIE ALLEN

Eat not to dullness. Drink not to elevation.
BENJAMIN FRANKLIN

Statistics show that of those who contract the habit of eating, very few ever survive.
WILLIAM WALLACE IRWIN

The culinary art depends on the psychological state of society . . . wherever life is easy and comfortable, where the future is assured, it always experiences a considerable development. On the contrary, wherever life and its cares preoccupy the mind of man he cannot give to good cheer more than a limited place. Oftener than not, the necessity of nourishing themselves appears to persons swept up in the hurly burly of business not as a pleasure but as a chore. They consider lost the time spent at table and demand only one thing: to be served quickly.
ESCOFFIER

Eating and sleeping are a waste of time.
GERALD FORD

Appetite comes with eating.
FRANÇOIS RABELAIS

While it is undeniably true that people love a surprise, it is equally true that they are seldom pleased to suddenly and without warning happen upon a series of prunes in what they took to be a normal loin of pork.
FRAN LEBOWITZ

Gluttony is an emotional escape, a sign something is eating us.

PETER DE VRIES

He who distinguishes the true savor of his food can never be a glutton; he who does not cannot be otherwise.

THOREAU

If thou rise with an Appetite, thou art sure never to sit down without one.

WILLIAM PENN

Never eat more than you can lift.

MISS PIGGY

And now with some pleasure I find that it's seven; and must cook dinner. Haddock and sausage meat. I think it is true that one gains a certain hold on sausage and haddock by writing them down.

VIRGINIA WOOLF

Whenever I get married, I start buying *Gourmet* magazine.

NORA EPHRON

Marriage, as I have often remarked, is not merely sharing one's fettucine but sharing the burden of finding the fettucine restaurant in the first place.

CALVIN TRILLIN

I do not think that anything serious should be done after dinner, as nothing should be before breakfast.

GEORGE SAINTSBURY

Not only were the kitchen and servants' hall never visited by my mother, but they stood as far removed from her consciousness as if they were the corresponding quarters in a hotel. My father had no inclination, either, to run the house. But he did order the meals. With a little sigh, he would open a kind of album laid by the butler on the dinner table after dessert and in his elegant, flowing hand, write down the menu for the following day. He had a peculiar habit of letting his pencil or fountain pen vibrate just above the paper while he pondered the next ripple of words. My mother nodded a vague consent to his suggestions or made a wry face.

VLADIMIR NABOKOV

Give me the provisions and whole apparatus of a kitchen, and I would starve.

MONTAIGNE

At this point in the meal, the stomach was ready for serious eating, and I prepared beans with bacon grease, a dish I perfected in 1937 while developing my *cuisine du depression.*

The dish is started by placing a pan over a very high flame until it becomes dangerously hot. A can of Heinz's pork and beans is then emptied into the pan and allowed to char until it reaches the consistency of hardened concrete. Three strips of bacon are fried to crisps, and when the beans have formed huge dense clots firmly welded to the pan, the bacon grease is poured in and stirred vigorously with a large screwdriver.... The correct drink with this dish is a straight shot of room-temperature gin. I had a Gilbey's 1975, which was superb.

RUSSELL BAKER

If this is coffee, please bring me some tea; if this is tea, please bring me some coffee.

ABRAHAM LINCOLN

She sent for one of those short, plump little cakes called "petites madeleines," which look as though they had been molded in the fluted scallop of the pilgrim's shell. And soon, mechanically, weary after a dull day with the prospect of a depressing morrow, I raised to my lips a spoonful of the cake ... a shudder ran through my whole body and I stopped, intent upon the extraordinary changes that were taking place.

MARCEL PROUST

In the light of what Proust wrote with so mild a stimulus, it is the world's loss that he did not have a heartier appetite. On a dozen Gardiner's Island oysters, a bowl of clam chowder, a peck of steamers, some bay scallops, three sauteed soft-shelled crabs, a few ears of fresh-picked corn, a thin swordfish steak of generous area, a pair of lobsters, and a Long Island duck, he might have written a masterpiece.

A. J. LIEBLING

Wish I had time for just one more bowl of chili.
(alleged) dying words of
KIT CARSON

Take twelve to seventeen cockscombs, soak them in warm milk until the skins can be easily removed, wash them in cold water until the red pales to a surprising white, sprinkle them with lemon juice (Margaret used pickling liquor), roll the cockscombs in beaten egg, fry them briefly on both sides, and serve them, on rounds of celery root previously sauteed in butter, to any male who, as I did then, has trouble getting and keeping it up and displaying a cocky virility even when he has good reason to hang his head.

GUNTER GRASS

The primary requisite for writing well about food is a good appetite.

A. J. LIEBLING

I hated myself because I smelt of onions and meat, and I seriously considered suicide in the cistern which supplied the house.

LOUISE DE KOVEN BOWEN

Cooking is like love. It should be entered into with abandon or not at all.

HARRIET VAN HORNE

The greatest dishes are very simple dishes.

ESCOFFIER

What is patriotism but the love of the good things we ate in our childhood.

LIN YUTANG

When I was young and poor, my favorite dish was caviar accompanied by a half bottle of Bollinger. But repetition destroys any pleasure, gastronomic or sexual, and now I have no favorite dish having eliminated all my "favorites"! Now I like nothing better than a bowl of well made Scottish porridge, accompanied by a glass of good sweet milk, "supped" in spoonfuls in turn. Delicious, good and nourishing and without after-effects.

A. J. CRONIN

You have to eat oatmeal or you'll dry up. Anybody knows that.

KAY THOMPSON

I never see any home cooking. All I get is fancy stuff.
DUKE OF EDINBURGH

> There is in every cook's opinion
> No savoury dish without an onion:
> But lest your kissing should be spoiled
> The onion must be thoroughly boiled.
> JONATHAN SWIFT

The onion is the truffle of the poor.
ROBERT J. COURTINE

Potherbs in the autumn garden round the house
Of my friend the hermit behind his rough-cut
Timber gate. I never wrote and asked him for them
But he's sent this basket full of Winter Onions, still
Damp with dew. Delicately grass-green bundles,
White jade small bulbs.
Chill threatens an old man's innards,
These will warm and comfort me.
TU FU
from Juan Fang the Hermit on an
Autumn Day, Thirty Bundles of
Winter Onions. (795 A.D.)

Woe to the cook whose sauce has no sting.
CHAUCER

Cookery is become an art, a noble science; cooks are gentlemen.
ROBERT BURTON

He makes his cook his merit, and the world visits his dinner and not him.
MOLIÈRE

Plain cooking cannot be entrusted to plain cooks.
COUNTESS MORPHY

No artist can work simply for results; he must also *like* the work of getting them. Not that there isn't a lot of drudgery in any art—and more in cooking than in most—but that if a man has never been pleasantly surprised at the way custard sets or flour thickens, there is not much hope of making a cook of him.
ROBERT FARRAR CAPON

The art of cookery is the art of poisoning mankind, by rendering the appetite still importunate, when the wants of nature are supplied.
FRANCOIS DE SALIGNAC
DE LA MOTHE FENELON

Heaven sends us good meat, but the devil sends cooks.
DAVID GARRICK

There is no sight on earth more appealing than the sight of a woman making dinner for someone she loves.
THOMAS WOLFE

Zee always went naked in the house, except for the brassiere she wore when it was her turn to get dinner. Once, cooking French-fried potatoes in a kettle of boiling fat, she had come within an inch of crisping her most striking features.

G. S. ALBEE

The carp was dead, killed, assassinated, murdered in the first, second and third degree. Limp, I fell into a chair, with my hands still unwashed reached for a cigarette, lighted it, and waited for the police to come and take me into custody.

ALICE B. TOKLAS

My mother was a good recreational cook, but what she basically believed about cooking was that if you worked hard and prospered, someone else would do it for you.

NORA EPHRON

Custard: A detestable substance produced by a malevolent conspiracy of the hen, the cow, and the cook.

AMBROSE BIERCE

Never you tell, but I'll make her a pudding, a pudding she'll like, too, and I'll pay for it myself; so mind you see she eats it. Many a one has been comforted in their sorrow by seeing a good dish come upon the table.

E. S. GASKELL

Imagine, if you can, what the rest of the evening was like.
How they crouched by the fire which blazed and leaped
and made much of itself in the little grate. How they
removed the covers of the dishes, and found rich, hot
savory soup, which was a meal in itself, and sandwiches
and toast and muffins enough for both of them.

FRANCES HODGSON BURNETT

Many's the long night I've dreamed of cheese—toasted,
mostly.

ROBERT LOUIS STEVENSON

The height of luxury was reached in the winter afternoons
. . . lying in a tin bath in front of a coal fire, drinking tea,
and eating well-buttered crumpets is an experience few
can have today.

J. C. MASTERMAN

You don't get tired of muffins, but you don't find inspira-
tion in them.

GEORGE BERNARD SHAW

The smell of buttered toast simply talked to Toad, and
with no uncertain voice; talked of warm kitchens, of
breakfasts on bright frosty mornings, of cosy parlour
firesides on winter evenings, when one's ramble was over
and slippered feet were propped on the fender; of the
purring of contented cats, and the twitter of sleepy
canaries.

KENNETH GRAHAME

They fried the fish with bacon and were astonished; for no fish had ever seemed so delicious before. They did not know that the quicker a fresh water fish is on the fire after he is caught the better he is; and they reflected little upon what a sauce open air sleeping, open air exercise, bathing, and a large ingredient of hunger makes, too.

MARK TWAIN

I am one who eats his breakfast gazing at morning glories.

BASHO

Few of us are adventurous in the matter of food; in fact, most of us think there is something disgusting in a bill of fare to which we are unused.

WILLIAM JAMES

When a man is small, he loves and hates food with a ferocity which soon dims. At six years old his very bowels will heave when such a dish as creamed carrots or cold tapioca appears before him. His throat will close, and spots of nausea and rage swim in his vision. It is hard, later, to remember why, but at the time there is no pose in his disgust. He cannot eat; he says, "to hell with it!"

M. F. K. FISHER

I say it's spinach, and I say the hell with it.

E. B. WHITE

"There's no such thing as bad food," Mama used to say. "There are only spoiled-rotten children."
SAM LEVENSON

Toast was a big item in my mother's culinary pharmaco-peia. At first it was served plain and dry, but that was soon followed by crisp, sweet cinnamon toast, then baby-bland toast that tasted soothingly of fresh air. Thick slices of French toast, crisp and golden outside but moist and eggy within, would probably come next, always topped with a melting knob of sweet butter and a dusting of confection-er's sugar. I knew I was close to recovery when I got the toast I liked best—almost-burned rye bread toast covered with salt butter.
MIMI SHERATON

The only emperor is the emperor of ice cream.
WALLACE STEVENS

Once in a young lifetime one should be allowed to have as much sweetness as one can possibly want and hold.
JUDITH OLNEY

Young misses whut eats heavy mos' gener'ly doan never ketch husbands.
MARGARET MITCHELL

. . . I would stand transfixed before the windows of the confectioners' shops, fascinated by the luminous sparkle of candied fruits, the cloudy lustre of jellies, the kaleidoscopic inflorescence of acidulated fruitdrops—red, green, orange, violet: I coveted the colours themselves as much as the pleasure they promised me. Mama used to grind sugared almonds for me in a mortar and mix the crunched powder with a yellow cream; the pink of the sweets used to shade off into exquisite nuances of colour, and I would dip an eager spoon into their brilliant sunset.

SIMONE DE BEAUVOIR

One glance at her and I knew at once the sort of things that Dorcas would cook, that Dorcas was born to cook. Never, in later life, have I sat down to dinner without saying to myself, "Ah! things look Dorcassy tonight!" or, "Alas! there is nothing Dorcassy here."

DON MARQUIS

And please don't cook me, kind sirs! I am a good cook myself, and cook better than I cook, if you see what I mean. I'll cook beautifully for you, a perfectly beautiful breakfast for you, if only you won't have me for supper.

BILBO BAGGINS to the Trolls in
J. R. R. Tolkein's *The Hobbit*

Like most fine cooks, M. Bouillon flew into rages and wept easily; the heat of kitchens perhaps affects cooks' tear ducts as well as their tempers.

A. J. LIEBLING

Did it matter, did it matter in the least, one Prime Minister more, or less? It made no difference at this hour of the night to Mrs. Walker among the plates, saucepans, culenders, frying-pans, chicken in aspic, ice-cream freezers, pared crusts of bread, lemons, soup tureens, and pudding basins which, however hard they washed up in the scullery seemed to be all on top of her, on the kitchen table, on chairs, while the fire blared and roared, the electric lights glared, and still supper had to be laid. All she felt was, one Prime Minister more or less made not a scrap of difference to Mrs. Walker.

    VIRGINIA WOOLF

At the root of many a woman's failure to become a great cook lies her failure to develop a workmanlike regard for knives.

    ROBERT FARRAR CAPON

She died with a knife in her hand in her kitchen, where she had cooked for fifty years, and her death was solemnly listed in the newspaper as that of an artist.

    JANET FLANNER (GENÊT) writing about
    the death of Mother Soret of Lyons whose
    "chicken in half mourning" was famous
    all over France.

Too many cooks spoil the brothel.

    POLLY ADLER
    A House is not a Home

What I love about cooking is that after a hard day, there is something comforting about the fact that if you melt butter and add flour and then hot stock, *it will get thick!* It's a sure thing! It's a sure thing in a world where nothing is sure; it has a mathematical certainty in a world where those of us who long for some kind of certainty are forced to settle for crossword puzzles.

NORA EPHRON

I believe I once considerably scandalized her by declaring that clear soup was a more important factor in life than a clear conscience.

SAKI

Better is a dinner of herbs where love is than a fatted ox and hatred with it.

PROVERBS, 15:17

Music with dinner is an insult both to the cook and the violinist.

G. K. CHESTERTON

Our Indian kill'd a Deer, & the other men some Turkeys, but the Indian begg'd very hard that our Cook might not boil the Venison & Turkey together, because it wou'd certainly spoil his luck in Hunting, & we shou'd repent it with fasting and Prayer.

WILLIAM BYRD

What is food to one may be fierce poison to others.
LUCRETIUS

Mrs. Beaver stood with her back to the fire, eating her morning yogurt. She held the carton close to her chin and gobbled with a spoon... "Heavens, how nasty this stuff is. I wish you'd take to it, John... I don't know how I should get through my day without it."
EVELYN WAUGH

Inhabitants of underdeveloped nations and victims of natural disasters are the only people who have ever been happy to see soybeans.
FRAN LEBOWITZ

A man who is rich in his adolescence is almost doomed to be a dilettante at table. This is not because all millionaires are stupid but because they are not impelled to experiment. In learning to eat, as in psychoanalysis, the customer, in order to profit, must be sensible of the cost.
A. J. LIEBLING

Obtain a gross of small white boxes such as are used for a bride's cake. Cut the turkey into small squares, roast stuff, kill, boil, bake, and allow to skewer. Now we are ready to begin. Fill each box with a quantity of soup stock and pile in a handy place. As the liquid elapses, the prepared turkey is added until the guests arrive. The boxes delicately tied with white ribbons are then placed in the handbags of the ladies, or in the men's sidepockets.
F. SCOTT FITZGERALD

I hate people who are not serious about their meals.
    OSCAR WILDE

There is good dripping toast is by the fire in the evening.
Good jelly dripping and crusty, home-baked bread, with
the mealy savour of ripe wheat roundly in your mouth and
under your teeth, roasted sweet and crisp and deep brown,
and covered with little pockets where dripping will hide
and melt and shine in the light, deep down inside, ready to
run when your teeth bite in. Butter is good, too, mind. But
I will have my butter with plain bread and butter, cut in
the long slice, and I will say of its kind, there is nothing
you will have better, especially if the butter is an hour out
of the churn and spread tidy.
    RICHARD LLEWELLYN

To eat figs off the tree in the very early morning, when
they have been barely touched by the sun, is one of the
exquisite pleasures of the Mediterranean.
    ELIZABETH DAVID

Beulah, peel me a grape!
    MAE WEST in the movie
    She Done Him Wrong

When one has tasted watermelons, one knows what an-
gels eat. It was not a Southern watermelon that Eve took;
we know it because she repented.
    MARK TWAIN

A cucumber should be well sliced, and dressed with pepper and vinegar, and then thrown out, as good for nothing.

SAMUEL JOHNSON

about the strawberry:
Doubtless God could have made a better berry, but doubtless God never did.

WILLIAM BUTLER

... poultry is for the cook what canvas is for the painter.

BRILLAT-SAVARIN

> Ripe 'Sparagrass
>   Fit for Lad or Lass
> To make their Water pass
> O, 'tis a pretty Picking
>   With a tender Chicken

JONATHAN SWIFT

Everything depended upon things being served up the precise moment they were ready. The beef, the bay leaf, and the wine—all must be done to a turn. To keep it waiting was out of the question. Yet of course tonight, of all nights, out they went, and they came in late, and things had to be sent out, things had to be kept hot; the Boeuf en Daube would be entirely spoilt.

VIRGINIA WOOLF

Appetite, a universal wolf.

SHAKESPEARE

Open thine eyes, and thou shalt be satisfied with bread.
PROVERBS, 20:13

The fricassee with dumplings is made by a Mrs. Miller whose husband has left her four times on account of her disposition and returned four times on account of her cooking and is still there.
REX STOUT

Strange to see how a good dinner and feasting reconciles everybody.
SAMUEL PEPYS

The cook was a good cook, as cooks go; and as cooks go she went.
SAKI

Beef is the soul of cooking.
MARIE ANTOINE CARÊME

Greater eaters of meat are in general more cruel and ferocious than other men.
JEAN-JACQUES ROUSSEAU

When mighty roast beef was the Englishman's food,
It ennobled our hearts and enriched our blood,
Our soldiers were brave and our courtiers good.
Oh! The roast beef of old England!
RICHARD LEVERIDGE

In England there are sixty different religions, but only one sauce.

VOLTAIRE

Roast Beef, Medium, is not only a food. It is a philosophy. Seated at Life's Dining Table, with the menu of Morals before you, your eye wanders a bit over the *entrees*, the hors d'oeuvres, and the things *a la* though you know that Roast Beef, Medium, is safe and sane, and sure.

EDNA FERBER

If my young master must needs have flesh, let it be but once a day, and of one sort at a meal. Plain beef, mutton, veal & chicken, without other sauce than hunger, is best; and great care should be used, that he eat *bread* plentifully, both alone and with everything else; and whatever he eats that is solid, make him chew it well . . . If he at any time calls for victuals between meals, use him nothing but *dry bread*. If he be hungry more than wanton, *bread* alone will down; and if he be not hungry, 'tis not fit he should eat.

JOHN LOCKE

Everything in a pig is good. What ingratitude has permitted his name to become a term of opprobrium?

GRIMOD DE LA REYNIERE

But I will place this carefully
fed pig
Within the crackling oven; and,
I pray,
What nicer dish can e'er be given
to a man?
AESCHYLUS

He must be roasted.... There is no flavor comparable, I will contend to that of the crisp, tawny, well-watched, not over-roasted, *crackling*, as it is well called—the very teeth are invited to their share of the pleasure at this banquet in overcoming the coy, brittle resistance—with the adhesive oleaginous—O call it not fat! but an indefinable sweetness growing up to it—the tender blossoming of fat—fat cropped in the bud—taken in the shoot—in the first innocence—the cream and quintessence of the child-pig's yet pure food—the lean, no lean, but a kind of animal manna—or, rather, fat and lean (if it must be so) so blended and running into each other, that both together make but one ambrosian result or common substance.
CHARLES LAMB

What a world of gammon and spinach it is, though, ain't it?
CHARLES DICKENS

Canning gives the American family—especially in cities and factory towns—a kitchen garden where all good things grow, and where it is always harvest time. There are more tomatoes in a ten-cent can than could be bought in city markets for that sum when tomatoes are at their cheapest, and this is true of most other tinned foods. A regular Arabian Nights garden, where raspberries, apricots, olives and pineapples, are always ripe, grow side by side with peas, pumpkins, spinach; a garden with baked beans, vines and spaghetti bushes, and sauerkraut beds, and great cauldrons of hot soup . . .

JAMES H. COLLINS
The Story of Canned Foods, 1924

They ate frozen meat, frozen fried potatoes and frozen peas. Blindfolded, one could not have identified the peas, and the only flavor the potatoes had was the flavor of soap. It was the monotonous fare of the besieged . . . but . . . where was the enemy?

JOHN CHEEVER

And God said: Behold I have given you every herb-bearing seed upon the earth, and all trees that have in themselves seed of their own kind, to be your meat.

GENESIS, 1:29

The near end of the street was rather dark and had mostly vegetable shops. Abundance of vegetables—piles of white and green fennel, like celery, and great sheaves of young, purplish, sea-dust-coloured artichokes, nodding their buds, piles of great radishes, scarlet and bluey purple, carrots, long strings of dried figs, mountains of big oranges, scarlet large peppers, a large slice of pumpkin, a great mass of colours and vegetable freshnesses . . .

D. H. LAWRENCE

The Norman takes his vegetables in the form of animals. "Herbivores eat grass," one hotel landlord told me. "Man, a carnivore, eats herbivores."

A. J. LIEBLING
Normandy Revisited

I won't eat anything that has intelligent life, but I'd gladly eat a network executive or a politician.

MARTY FELDMAN

Vegetarians claim to be immune from most diseases but they have been known to die from time to time . . . there are millions of vegetarians in the world but only one George Bernard Shaw. You do not obtain eminence so cheaply as by eating macaroni instead of mutton chops.

GEORGE BERNARD SHAW

It is wonderful, if we chose the right diet, what an extraordinarily small quantity would suffice.

GHANDI

I devoured hot-dogs in Baltimore 'way back in 1886, and they were then very far from newfangled . . . They contained precisely the same rubber, indigestible pseudo-sausages that millions of American now eat, and they leaked the same flabby, puerile mustard. Their single point of difference lay in the fact that their covers were honest Germean *Wecke* made of wheat-flour baked to crispness, and not the soggy rolls prevailing today, of ground acorns, plaster-of-Paris, flecks of bath-sponge, and atmospheric air all compact.

H. L. MENCKEN

Eggs of an hour, bread of a day, wine of a year, a friend of thirty years.

ITALIAN PROVERB

If pale beans bubble for you in a red earthenware pot
You can oft decline the dinners of sumptuous hosts.

MARTIAL EPIGRAMS
Book XIII

Red beans and ricely yours,
      Is the way LOUIS ARMSTRONG signed his letters.

Pray for peace and grace and spiritual food, For wisdom and guidance, for all these are good, But don't forget the potatoes.

JOHN TYLER PETEE
Prayer and Potatoes

Nor do I say it is filthy to eat potatoes. I do not ridicule the using of them as sauce. What I laugh at is, the idea of the use of them being a saving; of their going further than bread; of the cultivation of them in lieu of wheat adding to the human sustenance of a country . . . As food for cattle, sheep or hogs, this is the worst of all the green and root crops; but of this I have said enough before; and therefore, I now dismiss the Potato with the hope, that I shall never again have to write the word, or see the thing.

WILLIAM COBBETT
A Year's Residence in the
United States of America, 1819

I am a great eater of beef, and I believe that does harm to my wit.

SHAKESPEARE

Any of us would kill a cow rather than not have beef.

SAMUEL JOHNSON

You can find your way across this country using burger joints the way a navigator uses stars. . . . We have munched Bridge burgers in the shadow of Brooklyn Bridge and Cable burgers hard by the Golden Gate, Dixie burgers in the sunny South and Yankee Doodle burgers in the North. . . . We had a Capitol Burger—guess where. And so help us, in the inner courtyard of the Pentagon, a Penta burger. . .

CHARLES KURALT

Mustard's no good without roast beef.
  CHICO MARX in the movie
  Monkey Business

Though regarded with disdain by the chic, and horror by the alfalfa-sprout crowd, hot dogs are flat—out wonderful. And versatile. Dripping with hot onions and ball-park mustard from a Sabrett man, they taste like New York; served in little cardboard doo-hickeys and called frankforts, they taste like America. They also make no unreasonable demands on the home cook.
  VLADIMIR ESTRAGON

Nothing helps scenery like ham and eggs.
  MARK TWAIN

Actually, the true gourmet, like the true artist, is one of the unhappiest creatures existent. His trouble comes from so seldom finding what he constantly seeks: perfection.
  L. BEMELMANS

Few among those who go to restaurants realize that the man who first opened one must have been a man of genius and a profound observer.
  BRILLAT-SAVARIN

I never eat in a restaurant that's over a hundred feet off the ground and won't stand still.

CALVIN TRILLIN

In the mornings, the waitress would wash down the floors of the hotel, and for that she would wear wooden clogs. At lunchtime she would take off the clogs and put on stockings and high-heeled slippers, a gesture of coquetry I can still see her performing. After she had pulled on the slippers, she would wash her hands at the spigot over a painted metal basin that was placed at the entrance of the dining room for the use of fastidious clients. She left an enduring impress on my life, although our relations were always impersonal. At my first meal at the hotel, I asked for a salad plate. She brought it to me, saying, with a superior smile, "Chacun son pays, chacun sa façon." I have taken my salad on my meat plate ever since, dabbling the lettuce in the leftover gravy.

A. J. LIEBLING

A recipe for fish baked in ashes: No cheese, no nonsense! Just place it tenderly in fig leaves and tie them on top with a string; then push it under hot ashes, bethinking thee wisely of the time when it is done, and burn it not up.

ARCHESTRATUS
Gastrology, 4th Century B.C.

Being becalm'd off Block Island, our people set about catching cod, and hauled up a great many. Hitherto I had stuck to my resolution of not eating animal food and on this occasion I consider'd . . . the taking of every fish as a kind of unprovoked murder . . . But I had formerly been a great lover of fish, and, when this came hot out of the frying-pan, it smelt admirably well. I balanc'd some time between principle and inclination, till I recollected that, when the fish were opened, I saw smaller fish taken out of their stomachs; then thought I, 'if you eat one another, I don't see why we mayn't eat you.' So I din'd upon cod very heartily . . . So convenient a thing it is to be a *reasonable creature*, since it enables one to find or make a reason for every thing one has a mind to do.

    BENJAMIN FRANKLIN

There is more simplicity in the man who eats caviar on impulse than in the man who eats Grape-Nuts on principle.

    G. K. CHESTERTON

Tell me what you eat and I will tell you what you are.

    BRILLAT-SAVARIN

> It's a very odd thing—
> As odd as can be—
> That whatever Miss T. eats
> Turns into Miss T.
>
>   WALTER DE LA MARE

Even as the eye glistened and the mouth began to water at the sight of a noble roast of beef, all crisp and crackly in its cold brown succulence, the attention was diverted to a plump broiled chicken, whose brown and crackly tenderness fairly seemed to beg for the sweet and savory pillage of the tooth. But now a pungent and exciting fragrance would assail the nostrils: it was the smoked pink slices of an Austrian ham—should it be the brawny bully beef, now, or the juicy breast of a white tender pullet, or should it be the smoky pungency, the half nostalgic savor of the Austrian ham? . . .

THOMAS WOLFE

Why so many different dishes? Man sinks almost to the level of an animal when eating becomes his chief pleasure.

LUDWIG VON BEETHOVEN

I remember his showing me how to eat a peach by building a little white mountain of sugar and then dripping the peach into it.

MARY McCARTHY

It is good for a man to eat thistles, and to remember that he is an ass.

E. S. DALLAS
writing about the artichoke, 19th Century

I like to imagine, in consummation and resolution of those jangling chords, something as enduring, in retrospect, as the long table that on summer birthdays and namedays used to be laid for the afternoon chocolate out of doors, in an alley of birches, limes and maples at its debouchement on the smooth-sanded space of the garden proper that separated the park and the house. I see the tablecloth and the faces of the seated people sharing in the animation of light and shade beneath a moving, a fabulous foliage, exxagerated, no doubt, by the same faculty of impassioned commemoration, of ceaseless return, that makes me always approach that banquet table from the outside, from the depth of the park—not from the house—as if the mind, in order to go back thither, had to do so with the silent steps of a prodigal, faint with excitement. Through tremulous prism, I distinguish the features of relatives and familiars, mute lips serenely moving in forgotten speech. I see the steam of the chocolate and the plates of blueberry tarts. I note the small helicopter of a revolving samara that gently descends upon the tablecloth, and, lying across the table, an adolescent girl's bare arm indolently extended as far as it will go, with its turquoise-veined underside turned up to the flaky sunlight, the palm open in lazy expectancy of something—perhaps the nutcracker.

VLADIMIR NABOKOV

There was a particular kind of wheaten biscuit with a very pale pure unsweetened flavor—I am reminded now of the Host—which only my mother had the right to eat. They were kept in a special biscuit tin in her bedroom and sometimes as a favor I was given one to eat dipped in milk. I associated my mother with a remoteness, which I did not resent, and with a smell of eau de cologne. If I could have tasted her I am sure she would have tasted of wheaten biscuits... The wheaten biscuit remains for me a symbol of her cool puritan beauty . . .

GRAHAM GREENE

When from a long distant past nothing subsists, after the people are dead, after the things are broken and scattered, still, alone, more fragile, but with more vitality, more unsubstantial, more persistent, more faithful, the smell and taste of things remain poised for a long time, like souls, ready to remind us, waiting and hoping for their moment, amid the ruins of all the rest; and bear unfaltering, in the almost impalpable drop of their essence, the vast structure of recollection.

MARCEL PROUST

I do like a little bit of butter to my bread.

A. A. MILNE

Always it was a club sandwich, the toast brown and crisp, the turkey moist with mayonnaise, the bacon sharp and smoky. The sandwich sat in the center of the plate, each of its triangular quarters secured by a toothpick. Next to it, on a single leaf of Boston lettuce, were two small gherkins. I ate those first, getting them out of the way before starting on the milk. And then, either in solitary glory or with the kids whose families let them eat upstairs every day, I looked out over the boats rocking at their moorings and lazily worked my way through each triangle. The waiter called me "sir," the tablecloth was white—and I was very fond of sandwiches.

    VLADIMIR ESTRAGON

I have always maintained that there is nothing wrong with nursery food now that we are grown up and can have a glass of wine with it.

    ELIZABETH RAY

The rule is jam tomorrow and jam yesterday, but never jam today.

    LEWIS CARROLL

I said my prayers and ate some cranberry tart for breakfast.

    WILLIAM BYRD
    diary, 1711

We plan, we toil, we suffer—in the hope of what? A camel-load of idol's eyes? The title deeds of Radio City? The empire of Asia? A trip to the moon? No, no, no, no. Simply to wake just in time to smell coffee and bacon and eggs. And, again I cry, how rarely it happens! But when it does happen—then what a moment, what a morning, what a delight!

J. B. PRIESTLEY

The breakfast is the prosopon of the great work of the day. Chocolate, coffee, tea, cream, eggs, ham, tongue, cold fowl—all these are good and bespeak good knowledge in him who sets them forth: but the touchstone is fish: anchovy is the first step, prawns and shrimps the second; and I laud him who reaches even these: potted char and lampreys are the third . . . but lobster is, indeed, matter for a May morning and demands a rare combination of knowledge and virtue in him who sets it forth.

THOMAS LOVE PEACOCK

Give me a platter of choice finnan haddie, freshly cooked in its bath of water and milk, add melted butter, a slice or two of hot toast, a pot of steaming Darjeeling tea, and you may tell the butler to dispense with the caviar, truffles, and nightingales' tongues.

CRAIG CLAIBORNE

Adam ate some breakfast. No kipper, he reflected, is ever as good as it smells; how this too earthly contact with flesh and bone spoiled the first happy exhilaration; if only one could live, as Jehova was said to have done, on the savour of burnt offerings. He lay back for a little in his bed thinking about the smells of food, of the greasy horror of fried fish and the deeply moving smell that came from it; of the intoxicating breath of bakeries and the dullness of buns . . . He planned dinners, of enchanting aromatic foods that should be carried under the nose, snuffed and then thrown to the dogs . . . endless dinners, in which one could alternate flavour with flavour from sunset to dawn without satiety, while one breathed great draughts of the bouquet of old brandy.

EVELYN WAUGH

. . . What? Sunday morning in an English family and no sausages? God bless my soul, what's the world coming to, eh . . .?"

DOROTHY SAYERS

One morning in November I awoke at 6:30 A.M. and looked out on a gray landscape that would have dispirited Gustave Doré: palpably damp, lunar in its deleafed desolation, it made my bone marrow feel as though I somehow had extracted it and left it in a dish on the back step all night. It was one of those mornings when a man could face the day only after warming himself with a mug of thick coffee beaded with steam, a good thick crust of bread, and bowl of bean soup.

RICHARD GEHMAN

Omlettes are not made without breaking eggs.
ROBESPIERRE

A simple enough pleasure, surely, to have breakfast alone
with one's husband, but how seldom married people in
the midst of life achieve it.
ANNE MORROW LINDBERGH

My wife and I tried to breakfast together, but we had to
stop or our marriage would have been wrecked.
WINSTON CHURCHILL

The breakfast food idea made its appearance in a little
third-story room on the corner of 28th Street and Third
Avenue, New York City . . . My cooking facilities were
very limited, (making it) very difficult to prepare cereals.
It often occurred to me that it should be possible to
purchase cereals at groceries already cooked and ready to
eat, and I considered different ways in which this might be
done.
J. H. KELLOGG

So in our pride we ordered for breakfast, an omelet, toast
and coffee and what has just arrived is a tomato salad with
onions, a dish of pickles, a big slice of watermelon and two
bottles of cream soda.
JOHN STEINBECK
travelling in Russia

The Russian tourist in America is instructed to ask for the following in restaurants: "Please give me curds, sower cream, fried chicks, pulled bread and one jellyfish."
The Russian-English Phrasebook

To be a gourmet you must start early, as you must begin riding early to be a good horseman. You must live in France; your father must have been a gourmet. Nothing in life must interest you but your stomach. With hands trembling, you must approach the meal about which you have worried all day and risk dying of a stroke if it isn't perfect.
L. BEMELMANS

A true gastronome should always be ready to eat, just as a soldier should always be ready to fight.
CHARLES MONSELET

Anyone who wants to write about food would do well to stay away from similes and metaphors, because if you're not careful, expressions like "light as a feather" make their way into your sentences and then where are you?
NORA EPHRON

Without bread, without wine, love is nothing.
French proverb

I use the verb "to eat" here to denote a selective activity, as opposed to the passive acceptance and regular renewal of nourishment, learned in infancy. An automobile receiving fuel at a filling station or an infant at the breast cannot be said to eat, nor can a number of people at any time in their lives.

A. J. LIEBLING

A gourmet is a being pleasing to heaven.

CHARLES MONSELET

Greece—Splendid little American lunches in pasteboard boxes that we ate in plane: hard-boiled egg with salt and pepper, one beefspread sandwich, one cheese sandwich, one peanut butter and marmalade sandwich, one cookie, one small container of cut up peach and pear compote, one small bag of assorted fruit drops—with pasteboard cup for water.

EDMUND WILSON
The Forties

The Americans are the grossest feeders of any civilized nation known. As a nation, their food is heavy, coarse, and indigestible, while it is taken in the least artificial forms that cookery will allow. The predominance of grease in the American kitchen, coupled with the habits of hearty eating, and the constant expectoration, are the causes of the diseases of the stomach which are so common in America.

JAMES FENIMORE COOPER

I would rather live in Russian on black bread and vodka than in the United States at the best hotels. America knows nothing of food, love or art.

ISADORA DUNCAN

To as great a degree as sexuality, food is inseparable from imagination.

JEAN-FRANCOIS REVEL

First prepare the soup of your choice and pour it into a bowl. Then, take the bowl and quickly turn it upside down on the cookie tray. Lift the bowl ever so gently so that the soup retains the shape of the bowl. *Gently* is the key word here. Then, with the knife cut the soup down the middle into halves, then quarters, and *gently* reassemble the soup into a cube. Some of the soup will run off onto the cookie tray. Lift this soup up by the corners and fold slowly into a cylindrical soup staff. Square off the cube by stuffing the cracks with this cylindrical soup staff. Place the packet in your purse or inside coat pocket, and pack off to work.

STEVE MARTIN

The man in evening clothes dining with the napkin in his lap will eat only half as much food as a diner in evening clothes with his napkin in his collar. The former will not only be worrying about spotting his shirt bosom but about the remarks his wife will make if he does.

DAMON RUNYON

On Bearnaise Sauce: It frightens me! With it one might never stop eating. Merely reading the recipe arouses my hunger.

BARON BRISSE

Cauliflower is nothing but cabbage with a college education.

MARK TWAIN

The receipts of cookery are swelled to a volume; but a good stomach excels them all.

WILLIAM PENN

A fool that eats till he is sick must fast till he is well.

GEORGE WALTER THORNBURY

To eat is human; to digest, divine.

CHARLES T. COPELAND

Indigestion: A disease which the patient and his friends frequently mistake for deep religious conviction and concern for the salvation of mankind. As the simple Red Man of the Western Wild put it, with, it must be confessed, a certain force: "Plenty well, no pray; big belly ache, heap God."

AMBROSE BIERCE

Indigestion is charged by God with enforcing morality on the stomach.

VICTOR HUGO

Digestion: The conversion of victuals into virtues.
  AMBROSE BIERCE

Part of the secret of success in life is to eat what you like
and let the food fight it out inside.
  MARK TWAIN

I have never regretted Paradise Lost since I discovered
that it contained no eggs-and-bacon.
  DOROTHY SAYERS

A beatific smile spread over his face!
Man had tasted the oyster!
In half an hour, mankind was plunging into the waves
searching for oysters. The oyster's doom was sealed. His
monstrous pretension that he belonged in the van of
evolutionary progress was killed forever. He had been
tasted, and found food. He would never again battle for
supremacy. Meekly he yielded to his fate. He is food to this
day.
  DON MARQUIS

He was a very valiant man who first adventured on eating
oysters.
  THOMAS FULLER

In general, only mute things are eaten alive—plants and invertebrates. If oysters shrieked as they were pried open, or squealed when jabbed with a fork, I doubt whether they would be eaten alive. But as it is, thoughtful people quite callously look for the muscular twitch as they drop lemon juice on a poor oyster, to be sure that it is alive before they eat it.

MARSTON BATES

"Have sense," she said sharply, "lobsters are always boiled alive. They must be." She caught up the lobster and laid it on its back. It trembled. "They feel nothing," she said . . . She lifted the lobster clear of the table. It had about thirty seconds to live.
Well, thought Belacqua, it's a quick death, God help us all.
It is not.

SAMUEL BECKET

What's the use of watching? A watched pot never boils.

E. S. GASKELL

Your truffles must come to the table in their own stock. Do not stint when you serve yourself: the truffle is an appetite creator, an aid to digestion. And as you break open this jewel sprung from a poverty-stricken soil, imagine—if you have never visited it—the desolate kingdom where it rules. For it kills the dog rose, drains life from the oak, ripens beneath an ungrateful bed of pebbles . . .

COLETTE

The truffle is not an outright aphrodisiac, but it may in certain circumstances make women more affectionate and men more amiable.

BRILLAT-SAVARIN

If I can't have too many truffles, I'll do without truffles.

COLETTE

. . . an honest laborious Country-man, with good Bread, Salt and a little Parsley, will make a contented Meal with a roasted Onion.

JOHN EVELYN

It is not really an exaggeration to say that peace and happiness begin, geographically, where garlic is used in cooking.

MARCEL BOULESTIN

And most dear actors, eat no onions nor garlic for we are to utter sweet breath.

SHAKESPEARE

There is no question that Rumanian-Jewish food is heavy. One meal is equal in heaviness, I would guess, to eight or nine years of steady mung-bean eating. Following the Rumanian tradition, garlic is used in excess to keep the vampires away; following the Jewish tradition, a dispenser of schmaltz (liquid chicken fat) is kept on the table to give the vampires heartburn if they get through the garlic defense.

CALVIN TRILLIN

Garlic is the catsup of intellectuals.
UNKNOWN

The kitchen, reasonably enough, was the scene of my first gastronomic adventure. I was on all fours. I crawled into the vegetable bin, settled on a giant onion and ate it, skin and all. It must have marked me for life, for I have never ceased to love the hearty flavor of raw onions.
JAMES BEARD

You better come on in my kitchen
'Cause it's going to be raining outdoors.
ROBERT JOHNSON

. . . such a shelter as you would be glad to reach in a tempestuous night, containing all the essentials of a house, and nothing for housekeeping; where you could see all the treasures of a house at one view, and everything hangs upon its peg that a man could use; at once kitchen, pantry, parlor, chamber, storehouse, and garret; where you could see so necessary a thing as a barrel or a ladder, so convenient thing as a cupboard, and hear the pot boil, and pay your respects to the fire that cooks your dinner and the oven that bakes your bread, and the necessary furniture and utensils are the chief ornaments; where the washing is not put out, nor the fire, nor the mistress, and perhaps you are sometimes requested to move from off the trap door, when the cook would descend into the cellar, and so learn whether the ground is solid or hollow beneath you without stamping.
THOREAU

And what a stove it was! Broad-bosomed, ample, vast, like a huge fertile black mammal whose breast would suckle numberless eager sprawling bubbling pots and pans. It shone richly. Gazing upon this generous expanse you felt that from its source could emerge nothing that was not savory, nourishing, satisfying.

EDNA FERBER

Our kitchen today is a rich, intoxicating blend of past, present, and future; basically it belongs to the past, when it was conceived and constucted. It is a strange and im- plausible room, dodolike to the modern eye but dear to ours, and far from dead. In fact, it teems with life of all sorts—cookery, husbandry, horticulture, canning, plan- ning. It is an arsenal, a greenhouse, a surgical-dressing station, a doghouse, a bathouse, a lounge, a library, a bakery, a cold-storage plant, a factory, and a bar, all rolled up into one gorgeous ball, or ballup. In it you can find the shotgun and shell for shooting up the whole place if it ever should become obsolete; in it you can find the mo- lasses cookie if you decide just to sit down and leave everything the way it is. From morning till night, sounds drift from the kitchen, most of them familiar and com- forting, some of them surprising and worth investigating. On days when warmth is the most important need of the human heart, the kitchen is the place you can find it; it dries the wet sock, it cools the hot little brain.

E. B. WHITE

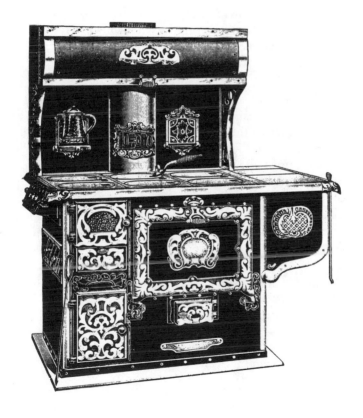

Six white pigeons to be smothered, to be plucked to be cleaned and all this to be accomplished before Gertrude Stein returned for she didn't like to see work being done.
ALICE B. TOKLAS

Salt is the policeman of taste: it keeps the various flavors of a dish in order and restrains the stronger from tyrranizing over the weaker.
MALCOLM DE CHAZAL

If it were not a pleasure, it would be an imperative duty to eat caviare . . . It is said that when sturgeon are in season, no less than two-thirds of the female consists of roe. It is certainly odd to think of a fish weighing perhaps 1,000 pounds being two-thirds made up of eggs . . . At such a rate of reproduction, the world would soon become the abode of sturgeons alone, were it not that the roe is exceedingly good . . .
E. S. DALLAS
Kettner's Book of the Table, 1877

Caviar is to dining what a sable coat is to a girl in evening dress.
L. BEMELMANS

Lazy fokes' stummucks don't git tired.
JOEL CHANDLER HARRIS

Fancy cream puffs so soon after breakfast. The very idea made one shudder. All the same, two minutes later Jose and Laura were licking their fingers with that absorbed inward look that comes only from whipped cream.

KATHERINE MANSFIELD

There he got out the luncheon-basket and packed a simple meal, in which, remembering the stranger's origin and preferences, he took care to include a yard of long French bread, a sausage out of which the garlic sang, some cheese which lay down and cried, and a long-necked straw-covered flask wherein lay bottled sunshine shed and garnered on far Southern slopes.

KENNETH GRAHAME

The whole Mediterranean, the sculpture, the palms, the gold beads, the bearded heroes, the wine, the ideas, the ships, the moonlight, the winged gorgons, the bronze men, the philosophers—all of it seems to rise in the sour, pungent smell of these black olives between the teeth. A taste older than meat, older than wine. A taste as old as cold water.

LAWRENCE DURRELL

Who will join me in a dish of tripe? It soothes, appeases the anger of the outraged, stills the fear of death, and reminds us of tripe eaten in former days, when there was always a half-filled pot of it on the stove.

GUNTER GRASS

The kulebyaka (coulibiac) must make your mouth water, it should be voluptuous, so to say, in all its glory. As you cut yourself a piece of it, you wink at it, and, your heart overflowing with delight, you let your fingers pass over it. . . Then you start eating it, and the butter drips like large tears, and the stuffing is succulent, luscious, there are eggs in it . . . and onions . . . Yes, yes, you eat two pieces of kulebyaka at once . . . but the third piece you reserve for the soup . . .

 ANTON CHEKHOV

My family dumplings are sleek and seductive, yet stout and masculine. They taste of meat, yet of flour. They are wet, yet they are dry. They have weight, but they are light. Airy, yet substantial. Earth, air, fire, water; velvet and elastic! Meat, wheat and magic! They are our family glory!

 ROBERT P. TRISTRAM COFFIN

Honest bread is very well—it's the butter that makes the temptation.

 JERROLD

. . . an egg which has succeeded in being fresh has done all that can be reasonably expected of it.

 HENRY JAMES

Old people shouldn't eat health foods. They need all the preservatives they can get.

   ROBERT ORBEN

The Duc de Bourgogne (Louis XIV's grandson) and his two brothers had been taught the polite innovation of using a fork to eat with. But when they were invited to the King's table at supper, he would have none of it and forbade them to use such an instrument. He would never have had occasion to reproach me in the matter, for I have never in my life used anything to eat with but my knife and my fingers.

   from the correspondence
   of the Princess Palatine,
   sister-in-law to Louis XIV.

When the ducks and the green peas came we looked at each other in dismay; we had only two-pronged, black-handled forks. It is true, the steel was as bright as silver; but what were we to do? Miss Matty picked up her peas, one by one, on the point of the prongs, much as Amine ate her grains of rice after her previous feast with the Ghoul. Miss Pole sighed over her delicate young peas as she left them on one side of her plate untasted; for they *would* drop between the prongs. I looked at my host: the peas were going wholesale into his capacious mouth, shovelled up by his large rounded knife. I saw, I imitated, I survived!

   E. S. GASKELL

We are still on the chapter of peas . . . the impatience to eat them, the pleasures of having eaten them, the joy of having eaten them again, are the three questions which have occupied our princes for the last four days. There are ladies who, having supped with the King, go home and there eat a dish of green peas before going to bed. It is both a fashion and a madness.

MADAME DE MAINTENON
a lady to the court of Louis XIV

We could not lead a pleasant life,
And 'twould be finished soon,
If peas were eaten with the knife,
And gravy with the spoon.
Eat slowly: only men in rags
And gluttons old in sin
Mistake themselves for carpet bags
And tumble victuals in.

SIR WALTER RALEIGH

Nature will castigate those who don't masticate.
HORACE FLETCHER

All I ask of food is that it doesn't harm me.
MICHAEL PALIN

All millionaires love a baked apple.
RONALD FIRBANK

Almost every person has something secret he likes to eat.
    M. F. K. FISHER

How long does getting thin take? Pooh asked anxiously.
    A. A. MILNE

Poets have been mysteriously silent on the subject of cheese.
    G. K. CHESTERTON

A cheese may disappoint. It may be dull, it may be naive, it may be oversophisticated. Yet it remains cheese, milk's leap toward immortality.
    CLIFTON FADIMAN

Never commit yourself to a cheese without having first *examined* it.
    T. S. ELIOT

There never was such a goose. Bob said he didn't believe there ever was such a goose cooked. Its tenderness and flavor, size and cheapness were the themes of universal admiration. Eked out by apple-sauce and mashed potatoes, it was a sufficient dinner for the whole family; indeed, as Mrs. Cratchit said with great delight (surveying one small atom of a bone upon the dish) they hadn't ate it all at last! Yet every one had had enough, and the youngest Cratchits in particular were steeped in sage and onion to the eyebrows.
    CHARLES DICKENS

The cold truth is that family dinners are more often than not an ordeal of nervous indigestion, preceded by hidden resentment and ennui and accompanied by psychosomatic jitters.

M. F. K. FISHER

O, blackberry tart, with berries as big as your thumb, purple and black, and thick with juice, and a crust to endear them that will go to cream in your mouth, and both passing down with such a taste that will make you close your eyes and wish you might live forever in the wideness of that rich moment.

RICHARD LLEWELLYN

"Who inu hell," I said to myself, "wants to try to make pies like Mother makes when it's so much simpler to let Mother make um inu first place?"

HARIETTE ARNOW

I remember that at one time I saw two of my young mistresses and some lady visitors eating ginger cakes, in the yard. At that time those cakes seemed to me to be absolutely the most tempting and desireable things that I have ever seen; and I then and there resolved that, if I ever got free, the height of my ambition would be reached if I could get to the point where I could secure and eat ginger cakes in the way that I saw those ladies doing.

BOOKER T. WASHINGTON

Had I but a penny in the world, thou shoudst have it for gingerbread.

SHAKESPEARE

Let them eat cake!
    often, but incorrectly ascribed to
    MARIE-ANTOINETTE

Wouldst thou both eat thy cake and have it?
    GEORGE HERBERT

... and when dessert time came he himself brought to the table a wedding cake that drew exclamations from all. Its base was a square of blue cardboard representing a temple with porticoes and colonnades and adorned on all sides with stucco statuettes standing in niches spangled with gold paper stars. The second tier was a mediaeval castle in *gateau de Savoie*, surrounded by miniature fortifications of angelica, almonds, raisins, and orange sections. And finally, on the topmost layer—which was a green meadow, with rocks, jelly lakes, and boats of hazelnut shells— a little cupid was swinging in a chocolate swing. The tips of the two uprights, the highest points of the whole, were two real rosebuds.

GUSTAVE FLAUBERT

And the Quangle Wangle said
To himself on the crumpety tree
"Jam and Jelly and bread
are the best of foods for me."
    EDWARD LEAR

"A loaf of bread," the Walrus said,
"Is what we chiefly need:
Pepper and vinegar besides
Are very good indeed—
Now if you're ready, Oysters dear,
We can begin to feed."
But answer there came none—
And this was scarcely odd because
They'd eaten every one.
                LEWIS CARROLL

I smoked cigarettes and I had affairs with Christians. But I
never ate a Baby Ruth or drank a Coca-Cola.
    BETTY ROLLIN

. . . I met a keen observer who gave me a tip: "if you run
across a restaurant where you often see priests eating with
priests, or sporting girls with sporting girls, you may be
confident that it is good. Those are two classes of people
who like to eat well and get their money's worth.
    A. J. LIEBLING

All people are made alike.
They are made of bones, flesh and dinners.
Only the dinners are different.
    GERTRUDE LOUISE CHENEY

During the whole repast, the general conversation was upon eating. Every dish was discussed, and the antiquities of every bottle of wine supplied with the most eloquent annotations. Talleyrand himself analyzed the dinner with as much interest and seriousness as if he had been discussing some political question of importance.

LADY SHELLEY
describing in her diary a dinner
at Talleyrand's house.

My advice to you is not to inquire why or whither, but just enjoy your ice-cream while its on your plate,—that's my philosophy.

THORNTON WILDER

Let us eat and drink; for tomorrow we shall die.

ISAIAH. XVII, 13

> Some hae meat and canna eat,
> And some wad eat that want it;
> But we hae meat, and we can eat,
> And sae the Lord be thankit.
>
> ROBERT BURNS

As God is my witness, as God is my witness . . . I'm never going to be hungry again. No, nor any of my folks. If I have to steal or kill—as God is my witness, I'm never going to be hungry again.

SCARLETT O'HARA
in *Gone With the Wind*,
by Margaret Mitchell

Dinner at the Huntercombe's possessed only two dramatic features—the wine was a farce and the food a tragedy.

ANTHONY POWELL

At a dinner party one should eat wisely but not too well, and talk well but not too wisely.

W. SOMERSET MAUGHAM

Because he was dining alone, his cook assumed a simple meal would do but his error was quickly corrected when Lucullus responded, "What? Did you not know, then, that today Lucullus dines with Lucullus?"

PLUTARCH

> I write these precepts for immortal Greece,
> That round a table delicately spread,
> Or three, or four, may sit in choice repast,
> Or five at most. Who otherwise shall dine,
> Are like a troop marauding for their prey.

ARCHESTRATUS

I feel now that gastronomical perfection can be reached in these combinations: one person dining alone, usually upon a couch or a hillside; two people of no matter what sex or age, dining in a good restaurant; six people, of no matter what sex or age, dining in a good home.

M. F. K. FISHER

EDITOR'S NOTE: *The reader with responsive taste buds and memory will naturally recall many wonderful passages not included here — some omitted because of limited space and some because I did not know them. I would be delighted to hear about them.*

This book was produced for the publisher.
by Ray Freiman & Company
Stamford. Connecticut 06903

PUSHCART